How is this answering the ? of
when you stop?

Other volumes in the series:

The Morse Poetry Prize
Edited by Guy Rotella

JENNIFER ATKINSON

The *Drowned* *City*

THE 2000 MORSE
POETRY PRIZE
SELECTED AND
INTRODUCED BY
CARL PHILLIPS

Northeastern University Press
BOSTON

Northeastern University Press

Library of Congress Cataloging-in-Publication Data
Atkinson, Jennifer, 1955–
    The drowned city / Jennifer Atkinson ; selected and introduced by Carl
Phillips
        p.   cm.—(The 2000 Morse Poetry Prize)
    ISBN 1-55553-454-6 (acid-free paper)
    I. Phillips, Carl, 1959–   . II. Title.   III. Morse Poetry Prize ; 2000.
    PS3551.T57 D76   2000
    811'.54—dc21   00-058228

Designed by Ann Twombly

Composed in Weiss by Graphic Composition, Inc., Athens, Georgia. Printed and bound by Versa Press, East Peoria, Illinois. The paper is Glatfelter Offset, an acid-free sheet.

MANUFACTURED IN THE UNITED STATES OF AMERICA
04   03   02   01   00   5   4   3   2   1

for my parents and in memory of theirs

ACKNOWLEDGMENTS

The author gratefully acknowledges the editors of the following pub-
lications where these poems, some in earlier versions, first appeared.

Bellingham Review	St. Veronica's Day
Black Warrior Review	Before the Connecticut River
Crab Orchard Review	The End of Advent
Crazyhorse	Aubade with a Measure of Hopkins, a Fiddle Tune, and an Old Irish Hymn
Delmar	After the Wind; The Disfigurement of Shame; Inheritance; Letter from the Drowned City (II); Letter from the Drowned City (IV); October Rose; Still Life with Angel; World Without End
Field	The Feast of the Assumption; Open Ghazal; St. Magdalen's Day: A Composition in Watercolor, Graphite, and Most of a Line of Hart Crane
Image	Pietà
The Iowa Review	The Madonna of the Serpent
Manoa	In the Interim: A Novella; Otherwise; June Anniversary
Natural Bridge	By Water; Elegy for a Girl Raped in 1977
New England Review	Dry Ghazal; Ghazal from the Drowned City; Ghazal from the Drowned City: Lines Written Under the Gilt and Glass Mosaic Dome of All Saints Church
Notre Dame Review	Conturbatio, Cogitatio, Interrogatio, Humilitatio, Meritatio: Ghazal on the Five Petals of the Salt Spray Rose; From the Psalter
Pleiades	Stolen Honey
Phoebe	Kite-Flying
Poetry	Ancient of Days; Extradition; The Miraculous
Shenandoah	Mirage; Storm Warning; Three Years: A Composition in Gesso and Graphite

Sou'wester	August Elegy; Beaver Meadow Road; Haddam Meadows; Solstice Eve; Stillness Pond; Way Up in the Middle of the Air
Threepenny Review	And Sweetness Out of the Strong
The Yale Review	Nimbus

"The World in Solemn Stillness Lay" and "Pietà" appeared in *The Gatekeeper's Secret*, an anthology edited by Suzanne M. Hunt (LaCrosse, Wisc.: Genesis Press, 1998).

I would also like to thank Allison Funk, Jeff Hamilton, Roger Lathbury, Steven Schreiner, Jason Sommer, and, especially, Eric Pankey for their attentive reading and generous, always supportive friendship.

Contents

OH BAWD

Introduction

What happens when belief—as artistic ambition, as a lover's devotion, as faith in divinity—is met with a staggering indifference? This is the question that Jennifer Atkinson's *The Drowned City* seeks variously to answer, and to which the poems themselves, finally, elegantly, unflinchingly become the only appropriate answer, one that does not offer closure to its questions so much as a means of fashioning a life inside them. The collection reads like a landscape painter's book of hours, but the meditations associated with such a book here lead not to a bolstering of faith in God via an appreciation of God's works; rather, the speaker of these poems—the painter, the artist— has begun to doubt what she had trusted, the Transcendental belief that in nature can be found the necessary clues or markers of divinity that might instruct us and so bring us closer to divinity. But what if the clues themselves are random? Or, as Atkinson puts it (in "Nimbus"):

> How to heed as if instruction
> unmeant effects: the silver of abstinent vapor
>
> as opposed to the foiled sky of a baptistry dome?

What if art is only artifice—not a way to find truth in the natural world, but instead a means of imposing our longing for "oracular, inscaped symbol" *upon* the world, of treating the world merely as "fit contextual landscape/confirming personal narrative" ("Beaver Meadow Road")? In the wake of which understanding, one way to think of art, Atkinson suggests, is as a "flimsy kite" to be reeled in, an ignominious contrast to the "lustrous remembered swans—/frozen, pure, mute, aloof" ("Kite-Flying") whose flight the artist's kite can but aspire to; it will never match it.

As the kite is to the swans, so is art to the more difficult reality of a life. In the course of these poems, Atkinson shows us how, by extension, a faith in the body's instinct toward the giving and taking of pleasure cannot counter adequately the fact of rape; nor does love in and of itself—be it bodily or spiritual—ensure against betrayal by (or an indifference from) those to whom we have given our love. "Duty, my love," says Atkinson in "Letter from the Drowned City (III)," "is delusion. There is none." She seems to speak from the eponymous drowned city whose motto might well be these lines from "World Without End": "No pleas are heard here nor are wishes granted." I take the drowned city to be faith itself, in all its manifestations, and these poems I take as letters, as it were, from the one survivor of the flood—letters written as their writer glides grandly, not unpeacefully across the very waters that have both ruined and preserved in ruined state the only world the writer ever knew to believe in.

Such survival is not without its power, lovely and lonely, the power of wisdom that finally sees our condition clearly: "What is ours? All but the gnomon, the little thorned rose, anything like certainty" ("Sundial Ghazal"). Which is also to say there's an exhilarating freedom that becomes possible, a freedom beautifully apparent in Atkinson's masterful re-inventions of the ghazal in the triumphant final section of this book, and a freedom of intellect and intuition that governs every poem here. With each rereading, *The Drowned City* becomes even more exciting, engaging, astonishing—for its richness of music, its agility of mind, its exactingness of vision, its unswerving ability to locate "the silence between/illumination and when its echo catches up" ("What Happened Next"). With pleasure I congratulate Ms. Atkinson; her readers will, I hope, be many—and grateful for these poems.

CARL PHILLIPS

Three Years: A Composition in Gesso and Graphite

From the drowned marsh-island lumbers the osprey.

Low inland fog annulled the creek and byways, all
but the tallest, tasseled reeds. Like sleep

mist overtakes rank distance and detail,
near and far, the expanse of wind-

trampled salt hay, the stiff seed crowns
at the creek edge. What dream is this

that your refusal should lie so quiet,
your heart the palm-up concave of a clamshell?

What cold dream that only the osprey, hunting, wakes?

The Chester-Hadlyme Ferry: A Composition in Graphite, Crayon, and a Line (in English) of Montale

It's the randomness, the unmeant glums
And glimmers dashed off across
The water—
                    elegant glyphs,
Gestural hirogana
No one intended—
                    that tempts one most.

If this glimmer is a truce . . .

On the river's other it looks like
Darker, mackled side,
                    a dock
Identical to this one
Hums
          with the ferry's slow departure.

Wind-ragged, a wind sleeve fills,
Flags, fills
                    —an easy figure.
As is the butterfly unfolding
Its outsized paper wings.
                              See
How one is tempted?
                              Before
You know it, here it comes.
                                        The ferry
Revs up and backs its engines,
Plowing its wake to the dock.

Solstice Eve

Between the phosphorous green of Venus rising
And the dull glow of the descendent moon,
Night, oily black as a ship's tarred hull,
Sails on the wind through the channel—

Undredged, shallow. The keel drags bottom.

On the porch rail citronella candles hover.
Fireflies singe the tips of the grass blades,
While across the dunes—monotonous, mild—
The bay's pale breakers hiss and fizz.

Nothing goes forward—lag tide—not yet,

But the bat's blind forth-and-back overhead
Behind its string of high-pitched echoes.

St. Veronica's Day

As sheer as a glimmer, all day a blue haze
has warped across the taut frame of the sky.

Like a shuttle wound fat with slubbed, undyed
silk, a single cloud wefts a fine gauze.

From the belfry of the tallest cedar the mockingbird
rehearses its hearsay—avian proverbs

and gossip retold as gospel, as song.
The sun intact as always goes down,

while over the other horizon rises
a day-moon, pale monoprint of sunlight—

delible, scarred with error, dim
behind the veil, the raveling finespun shimmer.

St. Magdalen's Day: A Composition in Watercolor, Graphite, and Most of a Line of Hart Crane

Green rustlings, more-than-regal disregard
Riffles the stiff, clean leaves of the laurel
Like cards—impatient under the glint and glower
Of moonlight and shifting cloud banks.

The rain when it breaks breaks eight miles off:
Lightning faint at that distance like flashbulbs
—Blue-white—at a stranger's wedding. Passed over,
Untouched like Pharoah's daughters, like a field mouse

Under the owl's shadow, the great horned owl—
Silent, sated, sparing you out of indifference.

Otherwise

Whether sage-leaved or lowly,
a flutter of wings or of fricatives,

goldenrod or Aaron's serpent,
awe or Arabian hamza,

whether or weather,
mute or trumpeter,

River of Heaven or spilled skim milk,
it's all water under the drawbridge now.

Wade across to cordgrass and dunes
where the beach rose, rose

by habit, blooms
white on the rose quartz sand.

Otherwise, don't. Be like that—
uprighteous among the swash-drawn reeds.

Kite-Flying

Shall I reel in my flimsy kite—in,
down, to the clay-stained sand, the reeds
fractured and splinted with ice, snow
still couched in the dunes' steep lees?

The tide is past slack and turning,
draining back to the Sound, and the swans,
tawdry, molting, are rounding the petty
Connecticut headland to graze the rumpled

chase at the Westbrook creek mouth.
Not sublime, serene, regal
but starved, cautious, hissing, jealous,
the dominant male arches his neck,

clacks his beak, and drives a rival
back to the sea, where the wind
fills its unfurling wings, and it sails
as if weightless and inviolate—apart.

What of those lustrous remembered swans—
frozen, pure, mute. aloof,
or wheeling in wild, clamorous flight?
Gone. Undo the crossed kite-sticks: go home.

Aubade with a Measure of Hopkins, a Fiddle Tune, and an Old Irish Hymn

The guttural hiss of the great blue heron,
or the surd blur of dragonfly wings,

the tight-fisted pink of my baby's damp palm,
accusation and shame, that hailstorm,

a white pelt of salt, of chokecherry, let God
throw the first, *down roughcast, down dazzling* . . .

—moraine at the scoured ice-brink of waking.
All this—gravel and boulder; arctic

and tropic; garnet, shale, beach glass, shard, the jaw-
bone of a fox still tufted with gold

and silver-tipped fur, or so I will almost
in day-gaps and lapses remember

like an old tune, is it *Be thou my vision,
naught be all else* . . . or just *Turkey in*. . . .

The hay barn caved under the weight of snow,
the onrush, an onslaught, bright ice melt

slip of thaw between solid sleep and airy
day and if I die before you wake

forget the rest, complaints and plaited visions,
aspen of angels, archangels of

birches bowed under a dazzle, glitter, be-
come litter of ice once it snaps and

tears as the voice of the osprey attacking,
wings wide, the great heron whose hiss and

vinegar, dry-throated, daughterly cry un-

                                    drowns me . . .

Nimbus

All but expunged, sans serif, glossed over—
adagio without the cumulo-islands,

unhurried, unhesitant.
And all the etch and cross-hatch below—exact, distinct,

before and after, trial and error—irrelevant.
What do I know of *ever*, always at *way* and *means-to*,

fearing and courting delirium, repetition?
(At the risk of repeating myself . . .)

How to heed as if instruction
unmeant effects: the silver of abstinent vapor

as opposed to the foiled sky of a baptistry dome?
Below, in the before-

the-downpour, the totting up
of last night's tide wash—mermaid's purse and

tangled kite string:
how, where, therefore

finally a cloud too large to see the shape of

2

The Disfigurement of Shame

Fear, she tells no one who might believe her,
moves her. Not fear so much of pain—
after all, she knows her body will
accommodate and that torn flesh

heals: she has given birth. Not fear
of—the word is disfigurement—although
to be unfigured, unnumbered,
zeroed, is close. And she is not

unafraid of the weapons,
the back of the hand. But what moves her
—what makes her move or, rather, remain
immobile—is a horror of shame:

ignominy, a word whose form in her mind
is the bleached bloated kernel ground
somehow to what they call grits.
She ducks her head to avoid their eyes.

She would like to believe and believes
at times that what she fears is the aberrant
one. How else to lie down, to arch her back,
to scrape her teeth down a lover's earlobe?

Fear is a kind of god to her. And love.
The two contend. Superstitious
or call it faithful, she does not run.
She has the look, she thinks, of nonchalance.

Nor does she even, always, avoid the dark,
the corners masked with dense foundation plantings.
She walks with her fists balled in her pockets
thinking *not me, not me, not me*

in the belief that it must be someone.

Elegy for a Girl Raped in 1977

The shadow of a dogwood shudders
over the muddy ground in a wind
only wet skin would register. The petals—
not petals but bracts—chaste and symmetric
will not fall but fade as the season advances.

Chafed, it looks like, to a faint red
luster, witch hazel canes lean
across the path, a shortcut home.
Broken, their astringent scent subdues
a moment the muck and skunk cabbage.

At the crease of the ravine, a brook as thin
here as a girl's arm, there
the width of her hips, and wider beyond
a levee of scrub laurel, runs
on thaw. Ice scums the surface.

This no-man's-land, the crime scene, preserved
by virtue of its paltriness and ugly damp,
harbors nothing of her. Rain erases.
Loose hairs, snagged in a briar,
soon line like swansdown the nests of sparrows.

Stillness Pond

In August a sullen bog, tetchy,
algae-scummed, the haunt of dragonflies
and peep frogs, spatterdock and reeds,
Stillness all but disappeared
in long summer's leafed-out woods.

And in autumn's too when fallen leaves
papered over its surface and muted the flow
of its feeder spring. In spring a daunting
moat of sludge kept me away—that,
the bugs, and green distractions elsewhere.

But Stillness in winter glimmered silver,
like mica, an opal, the coin of the realm
revealed in the open palm of the woods—
irresistible. I'd sweep off the snow
and skate in tight repeating figure eights.

One year, the last before that woods
was cleared for house lots, I saw enlarged,
like dreamt, beneath the lens of the ice
a face—intent, blue-eyed, as pale
as shucked Silver Queen corn—familiar,

transfixed and estranged from the weathered world.

And Sweetness Out of the Strong

From the rocks—fire, sheen, sheer stealth
released to strength—the lioness
sprung, and huntress by hunted

(the hero) was stopped midflight,
wrung, wrecked, rent wholecloth, and left
to rot in the desert sun.

Three days passed. One imagines
a whirlwind of flies, spirals
of vultures, black grace reeling

down on the lion's updrafted stink.
But no. Or not only what
one would imagine occurred.

When Samson returned, he turned
back the plush tawny pelt (why?
to judge the work of the world?)

and found sweet geometry,
a full hive. There in the rank
gap in the lion carcass

a cold golden spirit whirred.
One imagines forgiveness
like that—honey to the brim

of the wound—impossible,
rich, a ruinous riddle,
worth (do you still think, my love?)

betrayal to taste again.

October Rose

Full-blown and frost-blackened,
its mealy, yellow, chestnut-meat—
heart I was going to say, *heart*
as in what's in the chestnut's cocklebur husk
and mahogany shell housing incognito
the prize and the reason, sweetness, it opens—
(so why not?) heart fades last.

Also the fragrance, more pollen
than petal, autumn than bloom,
persists, and sharper than ever
the thorn. However, whatever the shade—
claret, madder, maroon (remember
how the damson-red bud, unstruck match,
once lit, flared damask silk?)—, color burnt fast:

live embers slowed to sleet-doused
coal. The October rose, done-for, deposed
dowager majarani of the sideyard,
munificent Persian slumped on her cane,
uncrowned, desceptered, undeceptive,
now leans against my neighbor's fence,
the image of feigned indifference.

Stolen Honey

Once, Love, all Eros knew of bees

                                was honey

and music, a whir and dreamy hum

he thought the droning gears of transformation—

the breath of roses,

                              thin air, mere perfume,

bewitched by sing-song spells

or manufactured

                          (either way he didn't care)

into the honey

                      he loved so much he dared

(though when was anything sweet ever denied him?)

to break the hive's

                      white wax seal

and take

                what would have been given. Freely and in abundance.

Stolen honey isn't sweeter,

yet, Love, once stung himself

do you suppose young Eros thought twice

                          before

he chose a new mark and released

as if it were (was it?) welcome,

                  a dart

on the magic of his bow's

                    high sustained vibrato note?

In the Interim: A Novella

Indifferent herself but in deference
to the idea of his pleasure, she steps
from her clothes, stands herself at his window.

The floorboards underfoot are cool.
She waits. Outside, city roofs pitch and tip
about his expensive famous district's

renowned, green, oxidized-copper dome.
Still unseen,
she turns to his open Steinway piano,

rests her fingers on the keys,
then clicks her nails, not sounding a note,
across a phrase or so of Brahms, a piece

she played as a girl some ten years ago.
Her fingers still remember the prim arpeggios
of the right hand, that wide hard chord of the left.

She knows he expects a seduction—his of her—
dinner out then Balanchine or Balanchine then dinner,
and next the affair to officially start,

blaze, then end—or perhaps they marry.
She will surprise him. What does she feel?
Once she believed

in love uncompromised by trying,
by kindness, by anything so remote as strategy.
Barefoot as a lenten penitent, in the winter-dry dark

she stood at the mirror
(even then aware of the other aware of her)
and brushed her slack hair.

She could taste the briny static sparks
she cast. She loved. She knew
what she felt was love. Now?

In the next room his hands interrupt
the water on its way to the basin.
His cupped palms fill.

What has the loved to do with the love?
What has the lover to do?

Extradition

Among the green equatorial doldrums,
trivial calms and squalls, the frivolous
lunging about of the water, she imagined
herself, at ease, beyond responsibility's
jurisdiction, and directionless.
She pictured low waves and a dollop
of seafoam, thick sargasso terracotta
kelp, swank ceremonious sunsets,
the moon only apparently snared
in the rigging, and a lover,
she thought—why not?—she'd not
here deny herself some lover, a shadow
to swag the stateroom doorway.
To starboard, dimly starred the harbor
hardly pricked at the gloaming dark: her conscience
pastel, even pretty, like some Miami at a distance—

Unanchored, adrift, she hoped lost at sea,
absconded to a blue equilateral idleness
somewhere south of duty and customs,
she might now have whiled away the hours
humming *spinnaker, spindrift, spendthrift*—

Instead the Coast Guard helicopter
dropped from the clouds like a god machine
in all its halogen glory, its rehearsed
Miranda chorus, the regular thrum
of its whirligig wings, and the search beam,
don't be afraid, fixed its glare.
She dared not refuse the dangled ladder up.
Abandoned to its ballast of shadows,
her beloved boat tips.
Home she imagines her imagined self

returning charged, in custody, soon to be
released again to her own recognizance.
From on high, not yet to the port, she regards
the red and green running lights
of other craft, unapprehended,
blurring on toward Río.

Exceptions

Even at high tide Cormorant Rock
disrupts the heirloom pewter
                              gleam of the water,
pitted and polished in hazy sun.
                              Close-up
it seems that surface
                    all but disappears: we look down
through the outboard's shadow into the turbulent Sound,
sunlit, dim, estuarial
                    miles from the river,
moted nearly opaque
                    with plankton and inland silt.
Suspended bladder wrack or ragged dulse,
rockweed, and a pennant of kelp, its hold-fast
clenched to a broken shell,
                              appear beneath the gleam
equally ambered in submarine murk.

Beyond our bay, its rocks, and the charted sandbars—
Hens and Chickens, Long Sand Shoal
(aqua-blue on the nautical map,
                              but actually
underfoot, graveled and streaked with blackish clay)—
the bottom drops off
                    to the "old dumping ground,"
white on the map and keyed "discontinued . . . 1977."
Drifting over,
            we don't bother to fish,
instead drinking beer from the cooler,
                              talking
of friends a thousand miles away in a heat wave,

their loves
                    and children or childlessness, whether jealousy's
color is emerald, olive, or sea,
                                        the jellyfish
alongside the boat, symmetric, clear,
trailing its stinging medusa hair but rendered
on shore a formless cloudy glob,
our daughter,
                    the way at three or four she sang
through her hours,
                    our life, like a plotless opera,
the time I got lost out here in a fog,
how to cook the squash and eggplants for supper . . .

                    A bellbuoy
clanks more or less like music
                                        when we listen.
Surface and depth, glare and gloom, interrupt
one another as the wind comes up
                                        and the water gets choppy,
to reflect or reveal sky or dark or down,
as the waves would have it,
                                        a puzzled clarity
—flinders and shards of color and gray—

more or less like a painting, except . . .

June Anniversary

for Eric

1.

The salt marsh, a chartreuse plain, scotched with last year's
broken reed straw,
                  is split with the lazy backwards S of the creek,
a shallow *canale* that floods in the rain and full-moon
high tides, awash almost to the sea
                        and the unlit
wick of our backyard cedar. The egret departs
through the bars of the clouds.
                    Come twilight and fireflies
and the fog-white Firemen's Carnival searchlight,
and we're up on our private *altane*
                  looking out
on a Sargenty smear of pearl and dress silk,
                      olivesheen
and the vanishing stain of a passing car's taillights.

2.

Last year we spent this day in shopworn Cannaregio,
by the station, where the street stalls
seemed never to close
                and the gray aqueous air was laced
with gasoline, soy sauce, and garlic.

Our room was once a monastic cell.
Across the alley a widow
                who aired her black
slip on a rail at night
                and lifted the hood

27

from her finches' cage each morning
while dressing, we liked to think,
                              for church.
The birds sang on the sill.
Our shutters latched against the heat
all long late afternoon in bed.

Our last night in that city of gated lusters,
gloams and floods, a prettiness
we'd taught ourselves to disbelieve,
under the glare of the vendor's light,
                              hunks of coconut,
nacred, arctic, exotic, reprised
the otherness and recognition
                        tasted in a kiss,
the bride's dress
we'd seen awash like a wake on the flagstones.
The stain on our minds indelible:
                        her mouth when she rose
from the sacrament, darkened
to show through the veil
                        well before it was lifted.

3

Ancient of Days

We rested under the rude grape arbor. Its dusk-
Blue concord fruit pending, its palm-sized
Leaves sunlit, pale-veined, interrupted the sky.

The scent, a purple smear on the air—muscat,
Sultana—sweet beyond belief, did deceive:
The grapes' wan-green flesh was sour. You taught me

To burst the grapes in my mouth, spit out
The seedy sour meat, and suck the juice
From the puckered skins. We ate—

Or rather drank—our fill that afternoon.
And the catbird mewed from the firethorn.
And the sun dropped to its autumn low. Returned

Today to that arbor, its rafters in ruins,
Its vine canopy torn and dragging the wine-
And rain-stained table—your splendid pavilion

Is broken—I almost believed you would come home,
Unlatch the gate you shut fast behind you,
Forgiving, forgiven, prodigal god, but no.

The temple stands empty, unhaunted,
But for the drone of my words, and the bees.

Inheritance

Her orchard came into my keeping that year—
orchard and house, gardens, the flagged
path from the well. Next door an abandoned
farm, past fallow, its barn collapsed—
a cobwebbed paradise for field mice,
barn swallows, an owl, and, green blaze
by the hay chute, fern consuming the decay—

admonished like a parable from its unmown pasture
overgrown already with mare's tail
(the grass children call wheat),
with once-again wild tiger lilies
tall to the farmhouse door, and sunflowers,
almost petalless, seed-heavy, nodding
scarecrows born of past years' birdseed.

She had left me no instructions.
Beside that lapse I took for ruin,
I worked all summer to prop the fruit-
burdened branches, to mow, to water,
and in the end to harvest. I climbed
the trees, lodged the bucket among
the leaves and picked—for hours, days.

When she tended the orchard, I wondered,
what then did the apples—Winesap, Russet,
Northern Spy—all ripe so nearly
at once—come to? Next door
the one tree left, festooned
as if for Christmas with bittersweet vines,
bore fruit for the birds and squirrels.

All the baskets from the cellar full,
hundreds of apples crushed and sugared
down, a dozen jars of yellow

minted jelly on the sill, I stopped,
sated, sick, unable to pick
or stomach another apple. And still
the branches bent like dowsing rods.

The ground was littered with fallen fruit;
the air buzzed with cider and bourbon,
raisin and bees, and already the late
pears gave in, ripe, to the touch.
I ducked the fence to the neighbor's field—
not once before in those months,
summer to autumn, had I been lonely—

and looked back across to her domain.
Let the grass go, the fruit fall,
let frost and thaw and three or four
long rains follow, let wind
or raccoons work loose the latches
and next year her kempt, till now well-kept
lands, like her neighbor's, would surrender.

I understood she would not be returning.
The trees and gardens, the white house,
once her keep and her stronghold,
soon, I had thought, our home, was given
into my keeping. Winter to winter, fall
to fall without respite. In her disregard.
From across the fence I heard the apples

drop, unstinting, denting the earth.

By Water

Too wide to cross on a whim, too green,
the river this morning tempts anyhow,
tempts like solitude, like excess.

On the far side beyond the blooms and chill
whirlwinds of mist off the water
the last of last night's shadows smudge

the bluffs and docks, the silted shore
to an indistinct charcoal gamut of darks
for all the world like a wilderness,

a woods one enters to return from changed.

World Without End

She is one who never reached the lakeshore.
Distracted by the petty opulence
of red tulips unhinged in a heat wave,
by the bitter almond heart of the peach,
which she cannot not pry into; waylaid
by her own hard-won good habits, by trust,
by fear, by virtue of a girlish smile,
the rigors of a rushed domestic life,
she does not come down. Envisioning blue
water, blue flag iris in the shallows,
blue-black swallows, their arced wings notched with white,
she longs for the lake as a girl might long
for the starched white confines of a nun's tight wimple.

She does not have to renounce the world—
its monotonous cruelty, its sundry
incandescent birds, its noise, and its clouds,
its chronicle of griefs and spectacles.
She does not have to renounce her fears:
her possessions will remain hers alone.
She need not bow down or pray or cast coins.
No pleas are heard here nor are wishes granted.

Those who have come to stand on the lakeshore,
under the moon in one phase or another,
under the sun at one height or another,
soon forget the pine air, the clear water,
the level horizon of their pilgrim
destination. Soon they are gathering
loose driftwood and grapevines, conniving rafts
to gain access to the solitary
low off-shore island—rocky, fogged, undreamt of.

Way Up in the Middle of the Air

A goldfinch rocks a thistle stalk.
Sumacs flare at the edge of the clearing.

Held long enough in the mouth the words
of lament and mourning and woe are like honey.

The failing crabapple, past bloom, past green,
marooned with fruit too sour to harvest,

muses over its torn tulle shadow
halfway up the low hill to the house.

A sparrow hawk wheels overhead, silent,
underwings bright as it tips on an updraft.

August Elegy

So long unlived in, untended, the house
I'd have thought by now would have foundered
in high grass and rampant goldenrod.
I would have thought the years, the weather,
and my neglect—fruit left to rot
on the trees, snows and thaws uncleared
and unheeded, rooms left cold, unslept in,
undraped from the sun—would have mattered.

True, cobwebs span the hearth,
ragged, unstuck strands trailing
from the blackened brass andirons wrought
to look like tasseled sheaves of wheat
tied up with concord grape vines.
Swallows have nested under the eaves,
and morning glories—some wild, some
reseeds—snood the prize tea roses.

True, ripe—no, overripe—peaches,
pecked at and gnawed on, just lie there,
unpreserved, on the ground. And raccoon
shit, studded with red chokecherries
and blueberries from the hill beyond the garden,
smears the granite back step.
True, the garden is a tract of moldy hay
and the toolshed tarpaper roof has rucked.

But nothing's really changed by my delinquency.
The gardens and house are as hers as ever.
Where the bees have found a chink
in the chimney mortar and a gap behind
and between the fieldstone and the lapstraked boards
of the house, they've built a hive.
She would know how to smoke the droning
bees to sleep, pry loose

a board and break off like chocolate
hunks of dripping honeycomb—their trove.
She would know how to tempt the queen,
how to swarm the hive around a stick
and carry it off like a smouldering torch,
laggard bees like smoke behind her.
What if I let the bees go on
summer after summer after fall filling

with honey the gap between the outside
wall and the plaster? What if I
lived within the hum, behind
the untasted feast, sealed up? Already
I can hear the bees at work
thrumming their wings to cool the hive.
Perhaps I only imagine the drowsy
scent of nectar, flowers, and wax.

Beaver Meadow Road

Consider the argument below:
None of this matters—
not the overlooking chokecherry,
stunted, suckered, and briared

in asters and wild, purple blackberry canes;
not the low-slung lichen-scarred
hemlock or the rain-slicked evergreen
half-circle of laurels; not

the brook, runneled and black, fast
and loud, beside the road; not the road,
frost-heaved and winding
east to the forest, west toward the river;

not the mossed-over graves—none of it
—not unless all the rattletrap
paraphernalia, the stage props,
come in handy somehow in the drama,

whether as ways to move the heart:
she taught me the names of the flowers,
or the argument: *a bluejay lights on a cherry branch*
and gladly gorges on sour fruit;

or else as oracular, inscaped symbol:
the laurels, say, or *the broken gate*
or *the narrow road through the meadow;* or else
as a fit contextual landscape

confirming personal narrative:
There where the clear water skids over
the rocks and drops to that black
pool, I caught my first big trout, its eye

vacant, its glitter dulling.
My father tore the body open,
cut loose the ripe guts and rinsed:
pink flesh in chevrons along its spine. . . .

On the other hand, however, step
into the icy spring-fed brook, graveled
underfoot, slick around the shins, glared
in sunlight, patent black in shadow,

tracked with its several musics, and sensation
overcomes a moment the need for the words'
or the world's redemption by virtue
of utility—don't you think?

Before the Connecticut River

At her back the ruined orchard,
once her fathers' relied-upon riches,
once bearing, now barren, derelict, disowned,

she watches the river, her own disowned
river—wide, slow, sparked and charred
in evening light—and she feels rich

watching the spindled, spendthrift eddies, rich
with the noble grandeur of her own
loss, *hers*, of the sweet, wrecked orchard—

river-washed orchard, orchard of ought-to-be-autumn
riches, hers—that is, hers to disown.

The End of Advent

                        An ice storm glints
On the cinder path and the pear tree,
                                      on the clothesline
In its chaste majesty,
And the red-flagged mailboxes bunched on the corner.
Cold as clean as dry sugar
Tastes granular on the tongue. Brilliance
                                      like buckshot stings
Everywhere at once—
                        hark, hark, hark:
The seen world as ever shines . . .

Sometimes, in winter, when the ice-sheathed barbs of the holly
Glare as they do now,
And the spruce stands tall enough to stand for something
At the frozen back garden's verge,
                                      I catch myself dreaming
Down the pollarded steeple on the old Haddam church,
Burnt and rebuilt. I remember the way
                                    the deacons' wives
Whited out
            with lilies its fat altar cross at Easter,
The pollen on the petals, the tassels on the flags,
The Allelulias and Risens, the organ
                                declaring a "victory won."

Reverend McLared, who bent tree roots
Into gnarled, elegant walking sticks
And put up great batches of concord wine jelly
                                            in his spare time,
Labored to ease our minds
With John's "Whosoever believeth, etc.,"

Words he regretted, he told us at dinner,
Having preached in Burma decades before.

I drive out to the end of Filley Road where the cracked
Macadam narrows and the forest officially starts,
Where mountain laurel,
                          wind-stunted, ice-lacquered,
Slaps at the car-doors,
                          and head in a ways
Past the frozen fire pond, a picnic site, a pine stand
So shady that even in summer a wintry gloom
                                              persists.
There's nobody else around.
                          So who's to mind
If I sing to the pine and hardwood
                          solitude a carol
Gapped
        and bridged with botched, forgotten, and made-up words?

The sign's down, but I know the place
By its over-and-gone
                     and set-apart look:
Stone fences in a rubble, a rusty loop
Of barbed wire in a clearing
Lapped with the wax-green fern they call Christmas.

It's been thirty years since I was last here.
Forty since anyone stoked the fires or shoveled the ash
At the Cockaponsett Charcoal Works and yet,
                                    under a deadfall,
A broken white birch,
                     twiggy and tinseled with icicles,
I unearth a heap of half-burnt logs,
                          load a couple into the car,

43

Wipe my charry hands on my shirt for the sheer pleasure of it,
And, cold or not,
                    do not yet turn homeward.

Tomorrow will be Christmas Day.

There's no such thing as silence in the woods.
But through the sheer unsteady wind, jays, and way-off
A ranger's chain saw,
                    I hear a footfall,
                                        another, and turn.
The doe, faded dun, nervous
                    —no ghost—
Startles and crashes back among the shadowed trees
As if she were the stranger.

The world is no Advent calendar, its days
Gilt doors marked with cardinal numbers and symbols:
Holly, lily, charcoal, deer
To be prized open, one by one,
                    a lesson in patience.

And who would prefer it were so?

What Happened Next

For days for no good reason I've dreamt
of the Bodnath rice fields, flooded silver, the stupa
prayer flags sodden, dripping like laundry.
I at twenty-four, in love with the world,
leant on a bale of barley straw and listened
to my class recite in unison
in Tibetan prayer meter, loud,
over the pings and gongs of monsoon rain
on the warped metal roof, the principal parts
of regular English verbs.
            A snake zigzagged
through the open door and we all fell silent.
I can't remember what happened next.

Outside, the path coiled up around the hill
past chicken pens, the kitchen garden
thick in the rainy season mostly with okra
and aubergines, the Western monks' and some
lay-teachers' quarters, several mango trees
the boys took turns defending, nights, from monkeys.
The rest of the monastery/school compound—
temple, kitchen, dorms, spring—was down
around the other side.
            That afternoon-
of-the-snake, lightning must have, like wisdom's
supposed to, in one stroke divided the sky,
wind would have shaken the roof, old-fashioned
sound-effects thunder, and down a gully
beside our classroom, runoff spilled
in a muddy sluice and cascade from tree
root to rock, as usual.
            The dogs,
I want to say the puppy's name was Ananda,

snored and stank in the back. What if sensing
them and the boys (dressed as monks but only
as children wear blazers and kilts to St. George's),
the serpent raised its sleek, like circumcised, head,
tasted the air to make certain, and certain, withdrew?
Or Ananda the burly, cowlicked pup, just then
struck by a nightmare, yelped, and the snake reversed,
bits of barley chaff stuck to its sinuous back.

It's not long before the things of the world
revert to story and symbol.
                              In the tale
of Buddha and the king cobra, the snake in the grass
unbeknownst to the man creeps up behind him,
rises out of its coils, and unfurls its royal
hood to shield from sun or monsoon rain
a man who's now, thanks to the snake, considered
a saint. Think how long the cobra swayed unseen,
silent advisor, sleepy-eyed,
while above the pair domed a great
fig tree.
                 Beside our temple steps
a giant fig (same species) grew,
its hollow trunk filled with prayers,
recopied fresh each year. I pressed its leaves
between the pages of my journal (gone—
stolen) and the Rexroth *One Hundred* . . .
a library book I forgot when I left
                                    to return.
The man, Buddha the Enlightened One
by the end of the story, vows to sit
and, through intelligence, persist, until
he has reached, as if a ripe fig on a high branch,
right knowledge, the end of suffering.
                                        Eve,
in another version of the story, one

whose snake (like the cobra) shivered through the creature
wayward in our classroom, nears her tree
from the margins of a paradisial orchard, a garden
gated off, a green take on the compound the prince-
turned-Buddha was born to. Nobody suffers—yet.
And the snake rises proud from its reptilian
haunches, winds its way up the forbidden
apple tree, and speaks. The woman stands
eye to eye with her snake, enjoying
its intelligence. Up to her knees
in unmown grass, watered by springs and evening
rains, hair tied back against the briar-rose and downswept
branches of the hemlock,
she listens to its sibilance as
she would any day to the mockingbird singing
its pastiche of allusions.
                                    She lifts her arm . . .

Monsoon winds had come to Nepal from the Vale
of Kashmir, obscuring all but the closest hill
in vaporous blue. It was as if the sky
erased the mountains. Falling rain blurred
each afternoon the dome and spire
of the whitewashed stupa, its painted-on,
androgynous eyes blinking in stormlight—

I don't remember what happened next

—lightning and thunder, flash and voice.
Perhaps the snake warped through the wet straw,
a blackish grosgrain ribbon among us
only long enough to reach an exit
on the other side.
                            Joy might last
that long, as long as the silence between
illumination and when its echo catches up.

Haddam Meadows

The future is tidal and salt, the present a rush to the brackish.

But here the river, green and silt past Haddam Island,
lags behind to let us memorize the crimp of the current
along the bank and exposed tree roots;
the eddy-spangled surface, a sandbar; the overgrown other side;
milkweed down, windblown, sunstruck,
lost in the glare way out over the channel;
the chill of the water, how it gloves your hand;
the wind at your neck like expensive silk,
the taut flight of the swallows out
and—blue wings and a flash of red umber—back,
out and back and out like a lure;
initials carved with the year on a driftwood log,
a ring-neck snake, head lifted, swimming, so tender.
And on shore its sheer, crazed, crumpled skin.

We sank a six-pack in the shallows and watched as the river
dimmed and scuffed. Evening opened like a cormorant's wing.

Liquid, the very word is *leaving*.

4

The Miraculous

Along the fishy, bait-stained pontoon docks,
mooring poles, cut saplings buried
deep in the tidal shallows, bloom, live,
despite the salt, despite their lopped-off
limbs, like some emblem of—what?
Faith, spring, resurrection? Like a long-gone
folkloric rite in which the wheaten Christ
thrown off a cliff to the sea was thought
to wake and then to drown. I tend
rather to think of Mary, the girl
whose husband was chosen by lot and by
prophecy: all those who would have her
were to bear cut staves to the temple.
The one whose stick, held before him
like a torch, leafed and flowered at once,
two seasons sung in one whole note,
would marry, though blind to the consequence,
the one conceived to conceive a god.
What did she feel first, that girl, when
Joseph, almost embarrassed to join the procession
of suitors, raised a branch as white
as his beard but with blossoms?
Fear and comfort, I think, not amazement.
How to amaze a girl whose dreams angels ennoble?
Fear, not at the thought of a stranger's
dry appropriating touch, but at the gaze
that met hers, that *saw* her, that knew, the same
long look one hopes was a solace.

Still Life with Angel

Given the girl, the intake of her
breath at a wingbeat, the parenthetical
hunch of her shoulders—yes, and her awe—
the perpendiculars, the particulars of the setup
brittle with rationale; given

the candlewick stiff with carbon,
the smoke abrupt in the upswept air
of the previous moment—it is always
a question of afterwards—who
would not hypothesize the upshot?

But back to the essential candle:
white taper, black wick, smoke
scrawled—a prescription—across
the blank tablet of the air.
The girl is listening for her name.

Outside it is autumn: the Michaelmas
daisies need staking, the hummingbird,
its famous throat a red match head,
rasps at a wall of convolvulus.
Or it is early winter: candelabra

ground pine burns under a heavy frost,
wick tips feverish with gold-flecked spores.
Or, more likely, it is spring
with a slicked iridescence
on the boatyard tarmac, the smoke

of a trash can fire zigzagging
skyward, wet, from the alley . . .
Close your eyes and what you remember,
yes, is composition and color—the weight
of gold-leaved plumes against the gravity

of blue—but also the story, don't you?—
the sexual *Jack be nimble*. And of Jill?
The slow, hiccuppy release of her breath.

The Madonna of the Serpent

Naturally she'd heard the story—
the woman born of bone and sleep,
after the pleasure of naming was over,
into a shady Alhambra of fountains and roses,
concentric paths from the river-hemmed woods
to the orchard and winding inward—a setup—
toward temptation at its pretty heart.
She had long considered Eve, unashamed and naked.
What suspense the Gardener must have felt
overseeing her aimless walks among
the lemon trees and apples, the grapes
wrinkling to raisins on the vine.
Until at last the device of the articulate
snake, the invention of fear and shame
resolve the conflict—will she? won't she?
—in a crowning envoi of curses, burning
like sunset through the arabesqued grillwork behind them.

Even so she froze, the serpent coiled
on a sunny rock—froze still and speechless
though a good stomp and outcry would have banished it.
The head, hardly separate from the body,
the wound-up length, leaden and scaled, sallow
beneath, slept unaware. She recognized
the lidded eyes and nostrils, the jawline
drawn as if with ink. Across
the floury dust, she saw the snake had left
its mark inscribed among her own.
The dreamy eyes slid open—blank,
unknowing, flat—but the tongue proved quick
like a snake. And the mouth. One glimpse and she knew
its yawn in an instant that felt, as she named it,

like anguish, like bodily pity, the nervous sting
of breast milk letting down in answer
to a baby's cry. The snake was gone.

The World in Solemn Stillness Lay

At midnight, however, however clear,
lit by impractical starlight and, in the East,
one wan signal flare,
all anyone looking would have seen,
bending low over the earth,
distracted by song and flight and the strenuous
pizzicati of the lyre, were shadows on shadow,
wind shapes as dark as the dark
in the closed womb of an uncut melon.

But in such a dark one might make out
in gradations of green and purple the velvety
plush of what must be there and so
the details resolve: to thatch, stone,
stool, bridle, brindled wool,
the ruffed iridescence at the wood dove's throat
as she coos, and the woman, hooded, wakeful—
the child in the feedbox beside her hidden,
hidden well, like embers in a haystack.

Mirage

Dates rained from a palm-high heaven.
The fig, as yet uncursed, leant down
to let its ripened teardrop fruit—green

and streaked maroon—dangle low in easy reach.
As low as the little carob, its leather pods
split open like wallets. As easy as

lifting a shirt to feed a hungry child.
Dragonflies stitched in and out among
the reeds, darning rents in the illusion.

I can't now and couldn't then
pretend I didn't know. I knew.
A leopard, shrug-shouldered, gaunt,

ducked through the thorny chaparral
to share the oasis of the afternoon—
there by the same path the angel

blazed for us. The evening star rose up
pale as an eyelid, a tooth, the sole
of a newborn's foot and we followed.

But a mile into twilight I looked back.
Darkness wavered in darkness: mirage.
Overhead the crescent moon. Do I

remember or have I imagined
the sleepy, lunar, leonine eye
half closing in animal pleasure?

The Wedding at Cana

Soon the horizon, now a figure
for *distance*, for *never*, the unwalked-on future,
will be underfoot, suddenly close

like a wind-forced cloud, like hard rain.
Her dress will drag that horizon,
where for an afternoon a storm has stalled,

hem, skirt, bodice soaked.
Heavy and spread wide, a weighted
fishnet meant to sink.

Pietà

1.

Imagine, Silence, an almond tree,
one among many blooming within
a widowed queen's cloistered garden.

The blossoms fade. The yellow leaves
lengthen, crease, and darken. Night
by night, the fruit takes flesh.

The branches bend. Before the harvest
a storm unlocks the orchard gate:
wind, then hail, wild and smooth

as sparrows' eggs, rains down.
And, Silence, all her trees and every
almond fruit but one on one

low branch—the only one
the queen's own hand can save—
is spoiled. It alone ornamental

now, illustrative, waxes full
before it's plucked at summer's
perfect hour and stripped of the syrupy

sun-stained flesh of the world,
flesh for the sake of the stone heart,
stone which must be broken too

to yield the fragrant, milky—what is it,
tell me, at the core of the core of the core
of the queer's own votive sorrow?

2.

Forgive me, Silence, whose laughter, whose cry,
whose first word, whose first breath
was my music, the song of my long solitude.

I used to wish you already dead.
I feared your death that much.

Storm Warning

A green wind come west to find me
Reading under the burnt and burning
Rafters of the evening sky brings

Rosemary, singed and resinous, from the garden.
I have loved the scent of lightning
And rain, the white scald of what felt

Like angelic regard. But these days—forgive me—
When I think of that struck pine
Charred and doused in the same storm,

Years ago in the yard, it reminds me
Less of Gabriel's monitory bough,
His second, mute Annunciation, death,

Than it does of the morning after:
"Thank God,' we said, meaning the rain,
"The fire went nowhere but out."

The Feast of the Assumption

The worn velveteen of the staghorn
sumac reddens and sours at the path's end;
evening flares and smoulders like a pine-knot torch.

Over the water or the east marsh
the bass line, its melody lost,
of some simple rock song thrums and thrums—

neighborhood kids in an open garage.
The imaged sky—moon woozy in a white fog,
stars arrayed to a moral purpose—

unfolds like a hinged triptych, a spectacle,
a huge drive-in movie screen lit up
before a distracted crowd. The marsh

beyond the sumac-guarded way to the farther
dunes bristles with reeds, tall and broken.
A mother's voice: *Mary-Kate . . . Mary-Katherine, home!*

5
The Drowned City

Dry Ghazal

Dry lightning struck the parched bay tree.
Ember and incense lit the branches like spring.

Like parchment sheaves of mica crumble. The dry cliffside reads
Like a stack of letters bound with ribbon—foxed, blurred,
  addressed to the dead.

What if the crow in her dry voice spoke the final coda?
Would I listen? Would I accept the words that fell from her beak
  like bread?

I've made a study of the stones: the greenish flesh of beryl, icy
  quartz,
Shale and tourmalines, the dry, tight-fisted heart of the garnet.

Ask me no questions. I'll tell you no lies.
The dry wind turned. It rained. It rains. It's raining.

Letter from the Drowned City (I)

Now that the waters have risen,
Now that the boats have cast off or slipped their moorings,
Now that high tide leaves scallop shells friezed on the dull gold
    dome
And mourning palls of amber kelp snagged on the spires and spouts
    of All Saints Church,
Now that the others have fled,
I lodge like an owl, a swallow, a bat
In the mouldering, old mosaicked campanile,
Stranded in my refusals, the romance of a called farewell . . .

The very first day I stilled the bells.
And yet a resonant music, the chord that says the quarter-hour,
Hums, it seems, with every wave that breaks against the marble
    tower.

What years will pass as ours, hours as years in my drowned city,
An Atlantis of forgotten palazzos and orchards
(Lemons and pears thrust up from the waves as if on the palm of
    Neptune),
A Venezia of flooded kitchens and frescoes, wardrobes,
Mirrors, pearls in red velvet boxes, submerged
And silent. Swans scull overhead on the surface,
My love, as it is in heaven.

Ghazal from the Drowned City

A map of the stars is an icon.
The moon in the morning sky is a sign.

When you slept, I remember your skin smelled like almonds,
Awake like the spearmint and copper of stripped green birchwood.

With God as my witness, on earth as it is,
There's so little I dare say, less I dare to retract.

Our city is a miniature, a model, a plaything.
Its fabled grandeur reconfected in marzipan and meringue.

Night, day. I had forgotten the burnt-down taper
Of waiting, the purple-robed advent of cold.

Letter from the Drowned City (II)

All day I wander at no one's invitation,

                                  trespassing

in our once-beloved

                            abandoned city, through brackish precincts,

alluvial boulevards, sanctuaries of sloshing calm,

                                 the archives

where labeled shelves rise like cliffs

                              from the temperate fjords

                              of the flooded hallways.

What was it we learned to recite as children?
As we forgive those who trespass against us?

Late—too late to save them all—I remembered

                              and unlocked

the zoo gates and cages, unleashed the pent-up,

                            corralled,

                            marooned,

broke open the arabesque aviary,

                            the thick panes of aquarium glass.

Let the Great Siberian Tiger lope
up the stairs to the parapet,

                            sprawl on the overlook,

and drag her tongue across her cowlicked, agate fur.

Let her drowse, half-moon eyes

                            half-shut, half-vigilant,

where once as Sunday tourists we came to take the view.

Ghazal from the Drowned City: Lines Written Under the Gilt and Glass Mosaic Dome of All Saints Church

I set myself adrift under the piecemeal, puzzled
Countenance of Christ. His benedictory palm is raised.

Sound carries across the water, especially after dark.
In the dawn cries of wayward gulls your words arrive rephrased.

The hours of quarantine—autumn to autumn—pass uncounted, slow
And more slowly, like drops off my shipped oars' blades.

In the silted gutters of the old courthouse, morning glories
Have sprouted and bloomed—a debt of blue repaid.

A flotsam of lemons, an oriole's nest, a dog asleep on the windowsill.
Who can keep strict account of all the tides have taken and given
    these days?

Ghazal at the Frayed Seam of Marsh, Creek, and Sun-Bleached Ocean

I turn but wherever I turn I can hear the thread whir through the
   wheel,
Whir and catch, whir and snag, a stuttered voice that will not quite
   break.

Your poppies will bloom for years unheeded,
A pictogram of prairie fire, back fire against the real flames.

Dragonflies or *darning needles?* Either way on doubled wings,
Singe or mend, rend or seal up—*liar beware*—the dusk-edge of day.

Every word is a struck match—the kiss and rasp
Of plosive and fricative, the gasp and cry of I, O, Ah, A.

Straw into gold, gold into straw.
How many days to divine your name?

Conturbatio, Cogitatio, Interrogatio, Humilitatio, Meritatio: Ghazal on the Five Petals of the Salt Spray Rose

Overturned on the tide, eyes pecked out, mouth and gills exposed
    in a clownish grin
On the waves, the skate's flesh wings flutter.

Dog whelk, periwinkle, shark's eye shells—worldly repose in a
    whorled paraphrase:
Zero, zero, zero. Zero from the lowest body whorl on up the
    columella spindle of the spire.

Renounce your silence. Say *succumb* and I will lie down, your left
    hand under my head.
Say *relinquish* and I will cede you the city. Hurry, my love. Day is
    near.

Under the sway of the sovereign moon and the rain, unwilled,
    under water, the rugged beach rose
Blooms among the languid seaweed white, its fruit ripe, votive,
    sour.

How could I forget the pale green glamour of fireflies, my baby's
    shriek of pain,
The gaze of a stranger, the color of honey, hunger, desire, fear, the
    taste of salt on your shoulder?

Ghazal from the Queen of Pentacles

Sovereign of solitude, I love the unsolved maze of the rain-gilded
   streets,
The vast hours of idleness, a wealth unheard of, unspent and
   unspendable, a beached sea chest of pirate gold.

Goldfinches perch on gargoyles' tongues; wrens lodge where moss
   transmutes marble,
Their nests a text of my gold and gray hairs, sloughed snakeskin,
   cellophane, tinsel, clay.

The flame-stained gold flesh of the peach—flush, plush, roughcast
   at the core,
Tastes of your voice, your mouth, long, gold-leaved, cicada-loud
   days.

All that glitters isn't dross: sunlight parsed through a covenant of
   raindrops,
Moonlight cast willy-nilly like pearls, like hail, like seed pearls, like
   hailstones.

My love, who are you to bribe and scare and tempt and test me?
   Let me lie down, grant me safe passage,
Doubloons on my eyelids, the tip of my tongue, and heaped in my
   open, upturned palms.

Love Song at the Keyboard of the All Saints Organ

The organ's leather bellows croon sage-green silty smoke,
A contrail of chords and mold as fine as powdered blush.

Swear to me, by the deer in the field, the cat in the alley,
The wren and the fish hawk, you will never forget me.

I renounced all I dared to live without for now and you
Being you took the rest. When you looked back

Your face was a blur, your raised hand a star,
The asterisk to a footnote: your touch, light and lavish.

Swear to me, by the lemon lily, the symmetry of an octave,
The buried bulb and the errant seed, you will never forget me.

Music like wine is a balm for love and loss alike.
Music like wine sooner or later crowns its lover with a headache.

Sooner or later the cloud of chords falls. Would you even know,
My bridegroom, me—my face, my body, under its veil—

Green hair, green eyelids, green lips and cheeks,
Green breasts with an undershadow of frost?

From the Psalter

According to the lily, praise is an arrow, a song
Loosed from the recurved bow of its petals.

According to the dove in the far-off pine, sorrows
Are credits in the ledger, tears pearls in an amethyst bottle.

According to the deer whom night has forsaken, best
Are the fields of half-ripe oats beset with quail easily startled.

According to the voice through the mask of feigned madness: I is
No more *I* than the star left is *star* when you lift the stencil.

According to the red field lily, praise is a serenade
That beguiles the lover and beloved alike: open your mouth and be
   grateful.

The Ghazal of Or and Or and Or

You, outside the portals and gates of leave and return,
Or I, lost though here still, which of us is the exile?

Which—the spiked chestnut shells, sprung and cast down, that
  litter
The shade beneath the tree, the blooming tree, or the scent loosed
  in a wide invisible spiral?

I thought loneliness was penance, that is, impermanent pain—
As in childbirth—not the disquiet of this undesired, *is it? is it*
  objectless? desire.

Why blue for *blue* and which? Day-sky, backlit and a little hazy, or
  night-,
Copper salt and black powder burst into and out of spectacular fire?

After the carols and carnival, in the morning, the children used to
  comb the beach
For spent, sodden shells, calling out *dragonfly, phoenix, palm tree, god's*
  eye.

After the Wind

Our winter's slow, punishing rains have ceased
their months-long hammer and shimmer and drone.
The flood will reach and pass its crest.

But like a pardoned prisoner just released,
I can't believe. Dazzled, I distrust the sun
or that winter's doldrum rains have ceased.

Your nod, your upturned palm—I'd not have guessed
how hot such cool images would burn. My refusal, mine alone.
Will the flood reach and pass its crest?

When Atlantis sunk, just one survived, a shipwrecked priest
adrift on a flotsam of kelp and mumbled orison.
His winter's just, punishing rains had ceased

their blinding squall but all the lone castaway noticed
was his solitude. For which, and rescue, he can't atone.
The flood had reached and passed its crest.

Forgiveness is given and taken whole, not pieced
together like cold mosaic. Love, come home.
Winter's slow replenishing rains have ceased.
The flood has reached and passed its crest.

Letter from the Drowned City (III)

Jonah lodged three days behind the ocean's baleen gate
—unnoticed, unswallowed, undrowned,
buried alive under the sod of a breaking wave.
Until death discovered him there forgotten.

The floodwaters have all but withdrawn to the sea.
Love, love, the world revealed is the world
we were taught to pray for, saying
Give, overhead and underfoot another day.

Everything I own I've stolen. There's no
giving it back—not the shiver of wind
over olive trees, the touch of your tongue, or
the pitch of my mother's voice raised in anger.

He woke with pearls in his mouth like cherry stones,
like ballast. Terns and swallows dragged their shadows
back and forth to weave an awning, back and forth
before the sun How else to repair the damage?

How else? Duty, my love, is delusion. There is none.
And yet like a dutiful daughter, I chose myself
the dress and the ring and the vows, determined
just the same to love the fetched-up stranger beside me.

A Narrative Ghazal

The story resumes: a column of salt, riddled by now
By rain, crumbles. Has even regret lost its flavor?

Graft, splice, tongue, cleft—scion to rootstock:
Hard quince (taste it?) blooms in the flesh of the pear.

Ask the daughters which is worse—luck's aftermath,
That furrowed plot of next and next, or sure white erasure?

Halfway from inland to gone, a washed-out pear-stump
Sprouts in a storm drain. Lodged. Caught out of the river.

I want to tell you my heart is broken. Forever.
But my heart is not—*was not*—quite broken. Ever.

Letter from the Drowned City (IV)

Once upon a time, there was a girl, Pearl, who was castaway on a far-off island, a deserted but not desert island, a tiny Serendip land inhabited by eagles and gazelles, migratory songbirds, swans and deep red flamingos, bats, turtles, fishes, and all manner of insects— all flying and swimming things, as you'd expect on such an island. All except the gazelles, that is, and the girl, whose provenance sets our story in motion.

The moon reads the island's face with a glance. One thunderhead shadows its entire terrain and yet this world will be all the world to that child.

Part wooded, part prairie, part marsh, the island persists. A brook tumbles out of green woods into gold prairie, slows and slogs through tasseled marsh grass, rides over the gravelly lip of the beach, and goes tamely into the sea. If you were to visit this island (assuming you could locate it with no map beyond the story and the astrolabe of your intuition), you could walk across the island's waist in just half a day. And yet it fits like a lucky charm in the right coat pocket of the Pacific Ocean.

Set the child adrift in a coracle. Let the wind blow, the tides rush, the waves ease her sleep. Let the cormorant guide her between the rocks, the porpoise gladden her journey. Let bread and fruit and rain sustain her from home to home, the island lagoon.

The boat foundered noisily on the gravel beach. At low tide the mudflats were lively with green crabs and seagulls, flamingos posed on one leg, egrets wading into the tidepools. *Bird*, she said and a flamingo revealed its eye and clacked its beak. Pearl climbed out of her boat, which, relieved of her weight, bobbed free and spun about. The waves broke and fizzed at her ankles; Pearl walked away. As a young child might or as anyone would who's been at sea, she walked unsteadily, unsteadily and dreamily away onto the prairie.

79

The eagle doesn't know her and so veers off low, its shadow quick and off-kilter on the grass. The gazelles freeze and stare at Pearl, a stranger among them. They let the wind riffle the stiff red hairs along their spines, the white hair-tufts at the tips of their ears. They watch her. The eagle re-ascends, stoops, its shadow, like its intent, focused on a particular fawn. *Deer*, Pearl says. The gazelles run, leaping as one body urged by one thought—to the woods. The eagle—talons first, wings wide—misses. The gazelles crash through to the underbrush. Pearl stands at the woods' edge looking up, enchanted, fanned by the eagle's winnowing wings.

Taken into the herd, Pearl learned the language of glance and gaze, chuff and sigh, nuzzle and tense. The gazelles showed her a fern bank by the brook where she and her sisters slept undisturbed through midday. They led her to a sandy oxbow where the whole herd could drink at once. The fawns let her pet them and they ate the tender shoots and leaves she held out in her open palm. The eldest gazelle, a straw-colored grandmother with complicated yellow horns, let Pearl ride on her back and without shaming her for her difference taught the child she was not gazelle. When grandmother died, Pearl kept the elder's horns, one for remembrance and one as a shovel to dig up roots.

Years passed. Pearl grew wise in the ways of the eagle and the ways of the herd, which grew large with Pearl as their guardian. Bored and hungry, the eagle learned to dive and eat fish like an osprey.

What will become of Pearl? Let the briar door close behind her, let the wind gust to disguise her footsteps, and the low sun wink out behind a cloud.

The prince of the western kingdom had heard the tale of the girl who was cast adrift. He hired a ship and a crew and bought provisions for a month, meaning to search only that long. The prince searched seven years before he dropped anchor in the island's tiny lagoon. There he found Pearl, the queen of her world, gathering eggs into a rough basket. She ran from the ship to the woods, ran with the gazelles, bounding about curiously in a joyous zigzag.

Pearl is not gazelle. She cannot really leap; she sometimes craves solitude like salt. And yet she wishes. She sees her sisters mate with the new males, swell and give birth to their slippery pale fawns and she wonders. In a dream the black-eared male tosses his head, nostrils flaring, as if she were gazelle, as if she might someday leap. But no. She kneels. He folds his spindly legs. She lays his head across her thighs and strokes his glossy fur.

Open Ghazal

Is the question always of entrance—into the body, into the earth?
Is the answer always in exit—out of the body, out of the earth?

When the thief says *open*, the secret door in the stone swings wide.
When the thief says *open*, the seed lodged at the hinge, the fissure,
   the fault in the quartz heart, sprouts.

Wind says *fog* for water, *dust* for earth.
I say *white cloud, dice clatter, honeycomb, thumb, thrum, brim, albeit, so be it,
   arrest* for you.

The night so hot. The moon so bright. Sleepless, at last patient, I
   keep watch in the garden.
Moths go about their business. Morning glories unpurse.

The revolving doors turn, their little air locks come unstuck,
Unsealed, like shut lips parting—I mean that sound.

Sundial Ghazal

After swanlight, shoal and shallows dispelled, the kingfisher hovers,
   unsteady, and falls.
Ungainly, big-headed, rust-stained, she falls through the visible into
   a viscous, moted, absinthine green.

What is ours? All but a pinfeather, milkweed fluff, the lily's pollen
   shadow.
What is ours? All but the gnomon, the little thorned rose, anything
   like certainty.

Rain, flood, withdrawal. Surf-broken wharves thrown about like
   yarrow, like pick-up sticks:
Who wouldn't see a puzzle of shift and reliance, glyph and
   correspondence—from, to. because of, between.

As if a basalt sky might slide into place—dull, sarcophogal,
   inscribed with stars and a demotic gloss.
A Rosetta Stone to read the world by, a grammar book, a decoder
   key.

I had been dreaming of rescue, as if I'd been kidnapped and held for
   ransom.
As if rescue meant salvage from solitude, that wide, salt, scalding
   cold sea.

A NOTE ON THE AUTHOR

Jennifer Atkinson grew up in Connecticut and was educated at Wesleyan University (B.A.) and the University of Iowa (M.A. and M.F.A.). Her first book of poems, *The Dogwood Tree*, was published by the University of Alabama Press in 1990. Her poems have also appeared in numerous journals, including *Field*, *Poetry*, *Delmar*, the *Yale Review*, and the *New England Review*. She teaches at George Mason University in Virginia.

A NOTE ON THE PRIZE

The Samuel French Morse Poetry Prize was established in 1983 by the Northeastern University Department of English in order to honor Professor Morse's distinguished career as teacher, scholar, and poet. The members of the prize committee are Francis C. Blessington, Joseph deRoche, Victor Howes, Ruth Lepson, Stuart Peterfreund, Guy Rotella, and Ellen Scharfenberg.